A Holistic Guide to Mental Health

C. P. Kumar
Reiki Healer & Author
Roorkee - 247667, India

Disclaimer

While every effort has been made to ensure the accuracy and completeness of the content in this book, the author cannot guarantee that the information contained herein is error-free, up-to-date, or suitable for every individual circumstance.

The author shall not be held liable or responsible for any errors or omissions in the content of the book, nor for any damages, or losses that may arise from any actions taken based upon the suggestions or contents presented in the book.

Readers are advised to use their own judgment and discretion in applying the information provided in this book, and to consult with qualified professionals before taking any action based on the contents of this book. The author disclaims any and all liability or responsibility for any actions taken or not taken based on the information contained in this book.

DEDICATION

To all those who strive for understanding, empathy, and compassion in the realm of mental health. May this guide serve as a beacon of knowledge and a source of solace for those in need.

In honor of the countless individuals who have bravely shared their stories, and those who continue to advocate for a world where mental well-being knows no stigma.

With heartfelt gratitude to the researchers, practitioners, and advocates whose tireless efforts pave the way for brighter tomorrows in mental health.

This book is dedicated to you - the seekers of understanding, the champions of empathy, and the architects of change.

C. P. Kumar

CONTENTS

PREFACE

In a world where the pursuit of physical health often takes precedence, the significance of mental well-being cannot be overstated. Mental health is not just the absence of mental illness; it encompasses a state of emotional, psychological, and social well-being that allows individuals to navigate life's challenges with resilience and vitality. It is a cornerstone of holistic health and essential for leading fulfilling lives.

This book, "A Holistic Guide to Mental Health", aims to illuminate the multifaceted nature of mental well-being, offering insights, understanding, and strategies to foster it in individuals and communities alike. Within these pages, we embark on a journey through the intricacies of the human mind, exploring its vulnerabilities, resilience, and the myriad factors that shape mental health.

From the very outset, we delve into the foundational concepts of mental health, acknowledging its paramount importance and dispelling the stigma that has too often shrouded discussions surrounding mental illness. We trace the historical evolution of attitudes towards mental health, from times of misunderstanding and marginalization to the contemporary era of advocacy and empowerment.

Each chapter in this book serves as a beacon of knowledge, guiding readers through the landscape of common mental health disorders such as anxiety, depression, bipolar disorder, schizophrenia, and PTSD. We unravel the complexities of these conditions, shedding light on their symptoms, impacts, and the pathways to healing and recovery.

Moreover, "A Holistic Guide to Mental Health" transcends the clinical realm to explore the interplay between genetics, environment, and mental well-being. It examines the unique challenges faced by children, adolescents, and adults in maintaining their mental health in the face of life's adversities. The significance of supportive relationships, effective communication, and community engagement in nurturing mental resilience is also underscored.

Furthermore, this book delves into therapeutic modalities, ranging from psychotherapy to medication, and explores the transformative power of support groups and holistic practices such as yoga, meditation, and mindfulness. It also calls attention to the imperative of advocacy and policy reforms to ensure equitable access to mental health care and eradicate stigma and discrimination.

As we embark on this exploration together, it is my fervent hope that "A Holistic Guide to Mental Health" serves as a beacon of hope, understanding, and empowerment for individuals navigating the complex terrain of mental well-being. May it inspire compassion, foster resilience, and ignite a collective commitment to building a world where mental health is valued, nurtured, and safeguarded for all.

With warmth and empathy,

C. P. Kumar
Reiki Healer & Author
Former Scientist 'G', National Institute of Hydrology
Roorkee - 247667, India
Web: https://www.angelfire.com/nh/cpkumar/virgo.html

Chapter 1. Introduction to Mental Health
Understanding the Importance of Mental Well-being

Mental health, often relegated to the shadows of societal discourse, is an essential component of overall well-being. In recent years, however, there has been a burgeoning acknowledgment of its significance, heralding a transformative shift in how we perceive and address mental health issues. This chapter serves as a gateway into the intricate world of mental health, aiming to elucidate its importance and the factors that contribute to its maintenance and deterioration.

The Human Mind

At the heart of mental health lies the human mind, a labyrinthine construct of thoughts, emotions, and perceptions. It is the crucible in which our experiences, beliefs, and aspirations converge to shape our reality. Understanding mental health necessitates a multifaceted exploration of the mind-body connection, acknowledging the symbiotic relationship between cognitive processes and physiological responses.

Mental Well-being

At its core, mental well-being encompasses a state of equilibrium wherein individuals can cope with the stresses of life, maintain fulfilling relationships, and realize their potential. It transcends the absence of mental illness, encapsulating resilience, adaptability, and a sense of purpose. Just as physical health is indispensable for vitality, mental well-being is fundamental for leading a meaningful existence.

The Stigma Surrounding Mental Health

Despite the strides made in mental health advocacy, stigma continues to cast a shadow over those grappling with psychological challenges. Deep-seated misconceptions and societal prejudices perpetuate discrimination, hindering individuals from seeking the support they desperately need. Dispelling the stigma surrounding mental health is paramount in fostering an environment of empathy, acceptance, and inclusivity.

The Interplay of Genetics and Environment

Mental health is a product of both genetic predispositions and environmental influences. While genetic factors confer susceptibility to certain conditions, environmental stressors, such as trauma, socioeconomic disparities, and societal pressures, can exacerbate vulnerability. Understanding this interplay is pivotal in elucidating the etiology of mental health disorders and tailoring interventions to address underlying mechanisms.

The Global Mental Health Crisis

In an era marked by rapid technological advancements and socioeconomic upheavals, the prevalence of mental health disorders has reached unprecedented levels. From anxiety and depression to more severe conditions like schizophrenia and bipolar disorder, the global mental health crisis transcends geographical boundaries, impacting individuals across diverse demographics. The pervasive nature of mental illness underscores the urgency of prioritizing mental health initiatives on a global scale.

The Ripple Effect of Mental Health

The ramifications of mental health extend far beyond individual suffering, permeating familial dynamics, workplace productivity, and societal cohesion. Untreated mental illness engenders a ripple effect, engendering a cycle of dysfunctionality and despair. By fostering a culture of mental health literacy and destigmatization, we can mitigate the adverse repercussions of untreated psychological distress and pave the way for collective healing.

Conclusion

In essence, mental health is the cornerstone of human flourishing, underpinning our capacity for resilience, empathy, and self-actualization. By embracing a holistic approach to mental well-being - one that transcends mere absence of illness - we can cultivate a society that nurtures and celebrates the inherent dignity and worth of every individual. In the subsequent chapters, we delve deeper into the historical, biological, and psychosocial dimensions of mental health, unraveling its complexities and charting a path towards holistic healing and advocacy.

Chapter 2. Historical Perspectives on Mental Health
From Stigma to Advocacy

Introduction

Mental health has been a topic of fascination, fear, and misunderstanding throughout human history. From ancient civilizations to modern societies, perceptions of mental illness have evolved significantly. This journey from stigma to advocacy reflects changing attitudes, scientific advancements, and the struggles of individuals with mental health conditions. Exploring the historical perspectives on mental health unveils a complex tapestry of beliefs, treatments, and societal responses that have shaped our understanding of the human mind.

Ancient Beliefs and Spiritual Interpretations

Throughout antiquity, mental illness was often attributed to supernatural forces or divine punishment. Ancient civilizations such as the Greeks, Romans, and Egyptians believed that mental disorders stemmed from displeased gods or demonic possession. Treatment methods included rituals, prayers, and exorcisms aimed at driving out evil spirits and restoring harmony to the afflicted individual. Despite the primitive understanding of mental health, these early societies laid the groundwork for recognizing the importance of mental well-being.

Middle Ages and the Rise of Asylums

The Middle Ages (5th century AD to the late 15th century AD) saw a shift in attitudes towards mental illness, as superstition gave way to more structured approaches. With the establishment of monasteries and hospitals, individuals with mental disorders found refuge in institutions designed to provide care and support. However, the treatment within these asylums was often cruel and dehumanizing, reflecting societal perceptions of mental illness as a form of moral weakness or divine punishment. Patients were subjected to harsh conditions, confinement, and sometimes even torture in the name of treatment.

Enlightenment and the Emergence of Psychiatry

The Age of Enlightenment (late 17th century to the late 18th century) brought about significant changes in the understanding and treatment of mental illness. The rise of empirical observation and rational inquiry led to the emergence of psychiatry as a distinct field of study. Pioneers such as Philippe Pinel and William Tuke advocated for more humane approaches to mental health care, emphasizing the importance of compassion, empathy, and therapeutic interventions. The establishment of moral treatment hospitals marked a pivotal moment in the history of mental health, challenging prevailing notions of insanity as a mark of moral depravity.

19th Century and the Medicalization of Mental Illness

The 19th century witnessed a shift towards medical explanations of mental illness, as advancements in neuroscience and psychiatry offered new insights into the workings of the human brain. The development of diagnostic categories and classification systems, such as the Diagnostic and Statistical Manual of Mental Disorders (DSM), laid the groundwork for modern psychiatric practice. However, the medicalization of mental illness also led to the marginalization of individuals with psychological disorders, reinforcing stereotypes and stigma surrounding mental health.

20th Century and the Deinstitutionalization Movement

The 20th century saw the rise of the deinstitutionalization movement, driven by concerns over the inhumane conditions and overcrowding in psychiatric hospitals. Advocates called for community-based care and support services aimed at integrating individuals with mental illness into mainstream society. While deinstitutionalization represented a significant step towards destigmatizing mental health, it also presented challenges in terms of funding, resources, and access to quality care. Many individuals found themselves caught in a cycle of homelessness, incarceration, and inadequate treatment as mental health services struggled to meet growing demands.

Mental Health Advocacy and the Recovery Movement

In recent decades, mental health advocacy has gained momentum, fueled by a growing recognition of the importance of mental well-being and the impact of stigma on individuals and communities. The recovery movement, which emphasizes empowerment, self-determination, and recovery-oriented approaches to care, has reshaped the landscape of mental health services. Peer support groups, consumer-run organizations, and anti-stigma campaigns have helped challenge stereotypes and promote understanding of mental illness as a treatable medical condition.

The Role of Legislation and Policy

Legislative initiatives such as the Americans with Disabilities Act (ADA) and the Mental Health Parity and

Addiction Equity Act (MHPAEA) have played a crucial role in advancing the rights of individuals with mental illness and ensuring equal access to treatment and services. These landmark laws have helped reduce discrimination and improve the quality of care for millions of Americans living with mental health conditions. However, challenges remain in terms of enforcement, funding, and addressing systemic barriers to mental health care.

Cultural Perspectives and Global Challenges

Cultural beliefs and societal norms play a significant role in shaping attitudes towards mental health and influencing help-seeking behaviors. In many cultures, mental illness is still stigmatized, leading to delays in diagnosis, treatment, and support. Addressing cultural disparities and promoting culturally sensitive approaches to mental health care are essential steps towards achieving equity and inclusion for all individuals, regardless of background or ethnicity. Moreover, global challenges such as poverty, conflict, and humanitarian crises exacerbate the burden of mental illness, underscoring the need for international cooperation and solidarity in addressing mental health issues on a global scale.

Conclusion

The historical journey from stigma to advocacy reflects the evolving understanding of mental health and the complex interplay of cultural, social, and scientific factors that shape our perceptions of mental illness. While significant progress has been made in challenging stigma, expanding access to care, and promoting recovery-oriented approaches, much work remains to be done. By continuing to raise awareness, challenge stereotypes, and advocate for policies that prioritize mental health, we can create a more inclusive and compassionate society where individuals with mental illness are treated with dignity, respect, and understanding.

Introduction

In today's fast-paced world, mental health disorders have become increasingly prevalent, affecting individuals from all walks of life. Understanding the symptoms and recognizing the signs of common mental health disorders is crucial for early intervention and effective treatment. This article delves into the intricacies of various mental health disorders, shedding light on their symptoms and providing insight into how to recognize and understand them.

Anxiety Disorders

Anxiety disorders are among the most common mental health issues globally, characterized by persistent feelings of worry, fear, and apprehension. Generalized Anxiety Disorder (GAD), Panic Disorder, Social Anxiety Disorder, and Phobias are some of the prevalent types of anxiety disorders.

Generalized Anxiety Disorder (GAD): Persistent and excessive worry or anxiety about a wide range of activities or events, often accompanied by physical symptoms such as restlessness, fatigue, and muscle tension.

Panic Disorder: Recurrent and unexpected panic attacks characterized by intense fear or discomfort, often accompanied by physical symptoms such as chest pain, shortness of breath, and dizziness.

: Intense fear or anxiety about social situations where the individual may be scrutinized or judged by others, leading to avoidance of such situations and significant distress.

: Persistent, irrational, and excessive fear of specific objects, situations, or activities, leading to avoidance behavior and significant impairment in daily functioning.

Symptoms of anxiety disorders include excessive worrying, restlessness, irritability, muscle tension, and difficulty concentrating. Individuals with anxiety disorders may also experience panic attacks, which manifest as sudden episodes of intense fear and physical discomfort.

Understanding the symptoms of anxiety disorders involves recognizing the pervasive nature of anxiety and its impact on daily functioning. It's essential to differentiate between normal levels of anxiety and clinically significant anxiety that warrants professional intervention. *Clinically significant anxiety* refers to anxiety symptoms that meet diagnostic criteria and cause distress or impairment in daily functioning.

Depression

Depression is a mood disorder characterized by persistent feelings of sadness, hopelessness, and loss of interest or pleasure in activities once enjoyed. Major Depressive Disorder (MDD), Persistent Depressive Disorder (Dysthymia), and Seasonal Affective Disorder (SAD) are common forms of depression.

Major Depressive Disorder (MDD): A mood disorder characterized by persistent feelings of sadness, hopelessness, and loss of interest or pleasure in activities, often accompanied by changes in appetite, sleep patterns, energy levels, and concentration.

Persistent Depressive Disorder (Dysthymia): A chronic form of depression marked by a depressed mood that lasts for at least two years, accompanied by symptoms such as low self-esteem, fatigue, poor appetite or overeating, sleep disturbances, and difficulty making decisions.

Seasonal Affective Disorder (SAD): A subtype of depression that typically occurs during specific seasons, most commonly in the fall and winter months, and is characterized by symptoms such as low mood, irritability, fatigue, weight gain, and increased sleep duration, with remission of symptoms during the spring and summer months.

Symptoms of depression encompass emotional, cognitive, and physical domains, including pervasive sadness, fatigue, changes in appetite or weight, sleep disturbances, and feelings of worthlessness or guilt. Depressive episodes can significantly impair an individual's ability to function and may lead to thoughts of suicide or self-harm.

Recognizing the symptoms of depression involves understanding the duration and intensity of mood disturbances and their impact on various aspects of life. It's crucial to differentiate between temporary sadness and clinical depression to provide appropriate support and treatment.

Bipolar Disorder

Bipolar Disorder is a mood disorder characterized by alternating periods of manic and depressive episodes.

Individuals with Bipolar Disorder may experience extreme fluctuations in mood, energy levels, and behavior, ranging from euphoric highs to debilitating lows.

Symptoms of Bipolar Disorder during manic episodes include elevated mood, impulsivity, grandiosity, decreased need for sleep, and excessive involvement in pleasurable activities. Depressive episodes are marked by symptoms similar to those of Major Depressive Disorder.

Recognizing the symptoms of Bipolar Disorder involves understanding the cyclic nature of mood disturbances and their impact on interpersonal relationships, work, and daily functioning. Early detection and intervention are crucial for managing the symptoms and preventing relapses.

Obsessive-Compulsive Disorder (OCD)

Obsessive-Compulsive Disorder (OCD) is characterized by intrusive, unwanted thoughts (obsessions) and repetitive behaviors or mental rituals (compulsions) performed to alleviate anxiety or distress. OCD can significantly impair an individual's quality of life and interfere with daily activities.

Symptoms of OCD include obsessive thoughts related to contamination, symmetry, harm, or unacceptable thoughts, as well as compulsive behaviors such as excessive cleaning, checking, counting, or arranging items. Individuals with OCD often experience distress and feel compelled to perform rituals to reduce anxiety.

Recognizing the symptoms of OCD involves understanding the irrational nature of obsessions and compulsions and their impact on daily functioning and relationships. Treatment for OCD typically involves cognitive-behavioral therapy (CBT) and medication to manage symptoms effectively.

Post-Traumatic Stress Disorder (PTSD)

Post-Traumatic Stress Disorder (PTSD) develops in response to exposure to a traumatic event or series of events, causing persistent distress and functional impairment. PTSD symptoms may manifest immediately following the trauma or appear months or even years later.

Symptoms of PTSD include intrusive memories or flashbacks of the traumatic event, avoidance of reminders associated with the trauma, negative changes in mood and cognition, and heightened arousal and reactivity. Individuals with PTSD may also experience emotional numbness and hypervigilance.

Recognizing the symptoms of PTSD involves understanding the impact of trauma on the individual's psychological well-being and daily functioning. Early intervention and trauma-focused therapy can help individuals process traumatic experiences and alleviate symptoms of PTSD.

Conclusion

Recognizing and understanding the symptoms of common mental health disorders are essential steps toward promoting early intervention, effective treatment, and improved quality of life for individuals affected by these conditions. By raising awareness and reducing stigma surrounding mental health issues, we can create supportive environments that encourage help-seeking behavior and foster resilience in the face of adversity. It's imperative to prioritize mental health and seek professional assistance when needed, as early intervention can make a significant difference in recovery and overall well-being.

Introduction

Anxiety disorders represent a spectrum of mental health conditions characterized by excessive fear, worry, and apprehension. They are among the most prevalent mental health issues worldwide, affecting millions of individuals regardless of age, gender, or background. Anxiety disorders can be debilitating, interfering with daily functioning, relationships, and overall quality of life. Understanding the complexities of anxiety disorders is crucial for effective management and treatment. In this article, we delve into the intricacies of anxiety disorders, exploring their manifestations, causes, and holistic approaches to mental well-being.

Defining Anxiety Disorders

Anxiety disorders encompass a range of conditions, including generalized anxiety disorder (GAD), panic disorder, social anxiety disorder (SAD), specific phobias, and others. While each disorder has its unique features, they share a common thread of excessive and persistent fear or worry that disrupts normal life activities. GAD involves chronic, excessive worrying about various aspects of life, whereas panic disorder is characterized by sudden, intense episodes of fear or panic attacks. SAD involves intense fear of social situations, while specific phobias entail irrational fears of specific objects or situations.

Manifestations of Anxiety Disorders

The manifestations of anxiety disorders can vary widely from person to person. Physical symptoms such as rapid heartbeat, sweating, trembling, and shortness of breath are common during anxiety episodes. Individuals may also experience cognitive symptoms such as racing thoughts, difficulty concentrating, and irrational fears. Emotional symptoms may include feelings of dread, apprehension, irritability, and restlessness. The severity and frequency of symptoms can fluctuate, often triggered by stressors or specific situations.

Causes and Risk Factors

The causes of anxiety disorders are multifaceted and may involve a combination of genetic, biological, environmental, and psychological factors. Genetics play a significant role, as individuals with a family history of anxiety disorders are more likely to develop similar conditions. Brain chemistry imbalances, particularly involving neurotransmitters such as serotonin and dopamine, can contribute to anxiety symptoms. Traumatic life experiences, chronic stress, and significant life changes can also increase susceptibility to anxiety disorders. Additionally, personality traits such as perfectionism and neuroticism may predispose individuals to excessive worrying and anxiety.

Holistic Approaches to Anxiety Management

Managing anxiety disorders requires a comprehensive and holistic approach that addresses the physical, emotional, social, and environmental aspects of well-being. While medication and therapy are commonly used treatments, integrating complementary and lifestyle interventions can enhance overall effectiveness.

Psychotherapy

Psychotherapy is a collaborative treatment approach between a therapist and a client, aimed at addressing psychological issues, emotional challenges, and behavior patterns through various therapeutic techniques and interventions, ultimately promoting personal growth, emotional well-being, and improved mental health.

Psychotherapy, particularly cognitive-behavioral therapy (CBT), is a cornerstone of anxiety disorder treatment. It focuses on identifying and changing negative thought patterns and behaviors to help individuals cope with challenges, manage symptoms of mental health disorders, and improve overall well-being.

CBT helps individuals identify and challenge negative thought patterns and beliefs associated with anxiety. By learning coping skills and relaxation techniques, individuals can better manage anxiety triggers and reduce the impact of symptoms on their daily lives.

Medication

Medications such as selective serotonin reuptake inhibitors (SSRIs), serotonin-norepinephrine reuptake inhibitors (SNRIs), and benzodiazepines may be prescribed to alleviate anxiety symptoms.

Serotonin Reuptake Inhibitors (SSRIs): A class of antidepressant medications that work by increasing the levels of serotonin in the brain by blocking its reabsorption, which helps alleviate symptoms of depression, anxiety disorders, and other mental health conditions.

Serotonin-Norepinephrine Reuptake Inhibitors (SNRIs): Another class of antidepressant medications that work by increasing levels of both serotonin and norepinephrine in the brain by blocking their reabsorption, used to treat depression, anxiety disorders, and chronic pain conditions.

Benzodiazepines: A class of psychoactive drugs that enhance the effects of gamma-aminobutyric acid (GABA), a neurotransmitter that inhibits brain activity. Benzodiazepines are primarily used to treat anxiety disorders, panic attacks, insomnia, muscle spasms, and seizures due to their sedative, hypnotic, anxiolytic, muscle relaxant, and anticonvulsant properties. However, they can be habit-forming and may lead to dependence if used improperly or for extended periods.

These medications can help rebalance neurotransmitter levels in the brain and provide temporary relief from anxiety. However, medication should be used in conjunction with therapy and lifestyle changes for optimal outcomes.

Lifestyle Modifications

Incorporating lifestyle modifications can have a significant impact on anxiety management. Regular exercise, adequate sleep, and a balanced diet contribute to overall well-being and resilience against stress. Mindfulness practices, such as meditation, deep breathing exercises, and yoga, promote relaxation and reduce anxiety symptoms. Limiting caffeine and alcohol intake can also help regulate mood and minimize anxiety triggers.

Social Support

Building a strong support network of friends, family members, and mental health professionals is essential for individuals coping with anxiety disorders. Social support provides validation, encouragement, and practical assistance during challenging times. Peer support groups and online communities offer opportunities for connection and shared experiences, reducing feelings of isolation and stigma associated with anxiety disorders.

Stress Management Techniques

Learning effective stress management techniques is vital for preventing anxiety symptoms from escalating. Time management strategies, prioritization, and boundary-setting help individuals maintain a sense of control over their responsibilities and commitments. Engaging in hobbies, creative outlets, and recreational activities fosters relaxation and enjoyment, counteracting the negative effects of chronic stress.

Conclusion

Anxiety disorders pose significant challenges to individuals' mental health and well-being, but they are manageable with the right support and interventions. By unraveling the complexities of fear and worry, individuals can gain insight into their anxiety triggers and develop strategies for coping and resilience. A holistic approach to anxiety management, encompassing therapy, medication, lifestyle modifications, social support, and stress management techniques, offers a comprehensive framework for addressing anxiety disorders. With patience, perseverance, and professional guidance, individuals can navigate the journey toward mental wellness and reclaim control over their lives.

Introduction

Depression is a complex and pervasive mental health condition that affects millions of individuals worldwide. It goes beyond mere feelings of sadness and can have profound effects on a person's thoughts, emotions, and behaviors. In this article, we will explore depression from a holistic perspective, examining its causes, symptoms, impacts, and potential treatments.

Understanding Depression

Depression is more than just occasional feelings of sadness or despair. It is a mood disorder characterized by persistent feelings of sadness, hopelessness, and a lack of interest in activities once enjoyed. While everyone experiences periods of sadness, depression is distinguished by its duration and intensity. It can interfere with daily functioning and significantly diminish one's quality of life.

Types of Depression

Depression is not a one-size-fits-all condition; it manifests in various forms, each with its unique features and challenges. Major depressive disorder (MDD) is the most common type, characterized by prolonged periods of intense sadness and loss of interest. Other types include persistent depressive disorder (dysthymia), bipolar disorder, seasonal affective disorder (SAD), and postpartum depression.

Major Depressive Disorder (MDD): A mood disorder characterized by persistent feelings of sadness, hopelessness, and loss of interest or pleasure in activities, often accompanied by changes in appetite, sleep patterns, energy levels, and concentration.

Persistent Depressive Disorder (Dysthymia): A chronic form of depression marked by a depressed mood that lasts for at least two years, accompanied by symptoms such as low self-esteem, fatigue, poor appetite or overeating, sleep disturbances, and difficulty making decisions.

Bipolar Disorder: A mood disorder characterized by alternating periods of depression and mania or hypomania. Depression symptoms in bipolar disorder are similar to those in MDD, while mania or hypomania involve periods of elevated or irritable mood, increased energy, impulsivity, and risky behavior.

Seasonal Affective Disorder (SAD): A subtype of depression that typically occurs during specific seasons, most commonly in the fall and winter months, and is characterized by symptoms such as low mood, irritability, fatigue, weight gain, and increased sleep duration, with remission of symptoms during the spring and summer months.

Postpartum Depression: A type of depression that occurs after childbirth, characterized by feelings of sadness, anxiety, and exhaustion, as well as changes in appetite, sleep disturbances, and difficulty bonding with the baby. It can affect both mothers and fathers and requires prompt treatment to prevent complications for both the parent and the child.

Causes and Risk Factors

The causes of depression are multifaceted and often involve a combination of genetic, biological, environmental, and psychological factors. Genetics can predispose individuals to depression, as can imbalances in brain chemistry and neurotransmitters. Traumatic life events, chronic stress, substance abuse, and certain medical conditions can also increase the risk of developing depression.

Symptoms of Depression

Depression can manifest in a variety of symptoms, which may vary in severity from person to person. Common symptoms include persistent sadness, feelings of emptiness or hopelessness, irritability, loss of interest in activities, changes in appetite or weight, sleep disturbances, fatigue, difficulty concentrating, and thoughts of death or suicide. These symptoms can significantly impair functioning in various areas of life, including work, relationships, and self-care.

The Impact of Depression

Depression exerts a profound impact on every aspect of a person's life, affecting not only the individual but also their family, friends, and broader community. It can lead to impaired cognitive function, decreased productivity, strained relationships, social isolation, substance abuse, and even physical health problems such as chronic pain and cardiovascular disease. Depression is also a leading cause of disability worldwide, contributing to significant economic and societal burdens.

Diagnosis and Treatment

Diagnosing depression involves a comprehensive evaluation by a mental health professional, including a thorough assessment of symptoms, medical history, and psychosocial factors. While there is no one-size-fits-all treatment for depression, various therapeutic modalities and interventions can help manage symptoms and improve quality of life. These may include psychotherapy (such as cognitive-behavioral therapy or interpersonal therapy), medication (such as antidepressants), lifestyle modifications (such as exercise and dietary changes), and complementary approaches (such as mindfulness and relaxation techniques).

Holistic Approaches to Healing

Holistic approaches to mental health recognize the interconnectedness of mind, body, and spirit and emphasize the importance of addressing all aspects of well-being. In treating depression, holistic interventions may include nutrition and dietary adjustments, regular physical activity, mindfulness practices, stress reduction techniques, social support networks, meaningful engagement in activities, and creative expression. These approaches aim to promote balance, resilience, and self-awareness while addressing the underlying causes of depression.

Prevention and Self-Care

Preventing depression involves adopting healthy lifestyle habits, managing stress effectively, cultivating supportive relationships, and seeking professional help when needed. Self-care practices play a crucial role in maintaining mental and emotional well-being, including adequate sleep, regular exercise, nutritious diet, time for relaxation and recreation, and engaging in activities that bring joy and fulfillment. Building resilience and coping skills can also help individuals navigate life's challenges and setbacks more effectively.

Support and Community Resources

Living with depression can feel isolating, but it's essential to remember that help and support are available. Support groups, peer networks, hotlines, and online communities provide valuable resources for individuals struggling with depression and their loved ones. Seeking support from friends, family, and mental health professionals can help alleviate feelings of loneliness and despair and foster a sense of connection and belonging.

Conclusion

Depression is a complex and multifaceted condition that affects millions of individuals worldwide. It is essential to recognize the signs and symptoms of depression, seek help when needed, and adopt holistic approaches to healing that address the mind, body, and spirit. By raising awareness, reducing stigma, and promoting compassionate care, we can work together to support individuals living with depression and create communities where mental health thrives.

Introduction

Bipolar disorder, previously known as manic-depressive illness, is a mental health condition characterized by extreme mood swings that include emotional highs (mania or hypomania) and lows (depression). These mood swings can be intense and disruptive, affecting a person's ability to function in daily life. In this article, we delve into the complexities of bipolar disorder, exploring its symptoms, causes, diagnosis, treatment options, and strategies for managing the condition effectively.

Understanding Bipolar Disorder

Bipolar disorder is a complex psychiatric disorder that affects millions of people worldwide. It is not just a matter of feeling happy or sad; rather, it involves dramatic shifts in mood, energy, and activity levels. Individuals with bipolar disorder may experience periods of elevated mood, known as mania or hypomania, during which they feel euphoric, energetic, and impulsive. These episodes are often followed by depressive episodes, characterized by feelings of sadness, hopelessness, and low energy.

Symptoms of Bipolar Disorder

The symptoms of bipolar disorder vary depending on the type and severity of the condition. During manic episodes, individuals may exhibit the following symptoms:

- Increased energy and activity levels
- Racing thoughts and rapid speech
- Decreased need for sleep
- Impulsive behavior and poor judgment
- Grandiosity and inflated self-esteem

Conversely, during depressive episodes, individuals may experience:

- Persistent sadness and feelings of worthlessness
- Loss of interest in activities once enjoyed
- Fatigue and low energy levels
- Changes in appetite and sleep patterns
- Suicidal thoughts or behaviors

Diagnosis and Classification

Diagnosing bipolar disorder can be challenging due to the complexity of its symptoms and the variability in mood patterns. Mental health professionals typically rely on a thorough assessment, including a detailed medical history, physical examination, and psychiatric evaluation. The Diagnostic and Statistical Manual of Mental Disorders (DSM-5) outlines criteria for diagnosing bipolar disorder and classifies the condition into several subtypes, including bipolar I disorder, bipolar II disorder, cyclothymic disorder, and others.

Causes and Risk Factors

The exact cause of bipolar disorder remains unclear, but it is believed to involve a combination of genetic, environmental, and neurobiological factors. Research suggests that individuals with a family history of bipolar disorder or other mood disorders may be at higher risk of developing the condition. Additionally, life stressors, traumatic experiences, substance abuse, and imbalances in neurotransmitters such as serotonin and dopamine may contribute to the onset of bipolar symptoms.

Treatment Approaches

Treatment for bipolar disorder typically involves a combination of medication, psychotherapy, lifestyle modifications, and support from mental health professionals. Mood-stabilizing medications such as lithium, anticonvulsants, and atypical antipsychotics are commonly prescribed to help regulate mood swings and prevent relapse. Psychotherapy, including cognitive-behavioral therapy (CBT), interpersonal therapy (IPT), and family-focused therapy, can help individuals better understand their symptoms, develop coping strategies, and improve interpersonal relationships.

Cognitive-Behavioral Therapy (CBT): A psychotherapeutic approach that focuses on identifying and changing negative thought patterns and behaviors to help individuals cope with challenges, manage symptoms of mental health disorders, and improve overall well-being. CBT is goal-oriented and typically involves teaching specific skills to address current problems.

Interpersonal Therapy (IPT): A short-term, structured psychotherapy approach that focuses on improving interpersonal relationships and communication skills to alleviate symptoms of depression and other mood disorders. IPT helps individuals understand and address problems in their relationships and social interactions, and it aims to improve the quality of these relationships.

Family-Focused Therapy: A therapeutic approach that involves the entire family in treatment to address issues related to mental health disorders, particularly mood disorders such as bipolar disorder and depression. Family-focused therapy aims to improve family communication, problem-solving skills, and support networks, while also addressing the impact of the disorder on family dynamics. It may involve education about the disorder, improving coping strategies, and enhancing family cohesion.

In addition to conventional treatments, lifestyle modifications such as maintaining a regular sleep schedule, engaging in regular exercise, practicing stress management techniques, and avoiding alcohol and drug abuse can play a crucial role in managing bipolar symptoms. Building a strong support network of family, friends, and mental health professionals can also provide valuable emotional support and encouragement during difficult times.

Challenges and Stigma

Living with bipolar disorder can present numerous challenges, including medication side effects, financial difficulties, relationship conflicts, and stigma associated with mental illness. Many individuals with bipolar disorder may face discrimination or judgment from others due to misconceptions about the condition. Overcoming stigma and seeking support are essential steps toward recovery and well-being.

Managing Bipolar Disorder

Managing bipolar disorder requires a comprehensive approach that addresses the physical, emotional, and social aspects of the condition. It is essential for individuals with bipolar disorder to prioritize self-care, adhere to their treatment plan, and communicate openly with their healthcare providers about any concerns or changes in symptoms. Developing a wellness toolbox that includes coping skills, relaxation techniques, and crisis management strategies can empower individuals to navigate the highs and lows of bipolar disorder more effectively.

Furthermore, maintaining a healthy lifestyle that incorporates balanced nutrition, regular exercise, adequate sleep, and stress reduction techniques can help stabilize mood and improve overall quality of life. Engaging in meaningful activities, pursuing hobbies, and cultivating supportive relationships can also foster a sense of purpose and connection, reducing feelings of isolation and despair.

Conclusion

Bipolar disorder is a complex and challenging mental health condition that requires ongoing management and support. By understanding the symptoms, causes, diagnosis, and treatment options for bipolar disorder, individuals can take proactive steps toward recovery and well-being. With proper treatment, self-care, and support, individuals with bipolar disorder can lead fulfilling and productive lives, despite the inherent challenges of the condition. Through education, awareness, and compassion, we can create a more inclusive and supportive environment for individuals affected by bipolar disorder and other mental health conditions.

Introduction

Schizophrenia is a complex and severe mental disorder that affects how a person thinks, feels, and behaves. It is often characterized by a combination of hallucinations, delusions, disorganized thinking, and impaired social functioning. Living with schizophrenia presents significant challenges for individuals and their families, impacting every aspect of their lives. In this article, we delve into the various dimensions of schizophrenia and explore the multifaceted challenges faced by those living with this condition.

Understanding Schizophrenia

Schizophrenia is not a singular condition but rather a spectrum of disorders with diverse manifestations and severity levels. The exact cause of schizophrenia remains elusive, but it is believed to result from a combination of genetic, environmental, and neurobiological factors. While the onset of schizophrenia typically occurs in late adolescence or early adulthood, it can affect individuals of any age.

Symptoms of Schizophrenia

The symptoms of schizophrenia can be categorized into three main groups: positive symptoms, negative symptoms, and cognitive symptoms. Positive symptoms include hallucinations, such as hearing voices or seeing things that are not there, and delusions, which are false beliefs that are firmly held despite evidence to the contrary. Negative symptoms involve a reduction or absence of normal functions, such as diminished emotional expression, social withdrawal, and lack of motivation. Cognitive symptoms encompass difficulties with concentration, memory, and executive functioning.

Challenges in Diagnosis and Treatment

One of the primary challenges in managing schizophrenia is accurate diagnosis. The symptoms of schizophrenia can overlap with those of other mental health conditions, leading to misdiagnosis or delayed diagnosis. Additionally, stigma surrounding mental illness may discourage individuals from seeking help or disclosing their symptoms, further complicating the diagnostic process.

Treatment for schizophrenia typically involves a combination of antipsychotic medications, psychotherapy, and psychosocial interventions. However, finding the right treatment approach can be a lengthy and trial-and-error process, as individuals may respond differently to various medications and therapies. Moreover, medication adherence can be a significant challenge due to side effects, cognitive impairment, or lack of insight into one's illness.

Impact on Daily Functioning

Schizophrenia can have a profound impact on various aspects of daily functioning, including work, relationships, and self-care. Many individuals with schizophrenia struggle to maintain employment or engage in meaningful activities due to symptoms such as cognitive impairment and social withdrawal. Relationships may also be strained by the unpredictable nature of the illness and the stigma associated with mental illness.

Self-care can become challenging for individuals with schizophrenia, as symptoms may interfere with basic tasks such as personal hygiene, nutrition, and medication management. In some cases, individuals may require support from family members, caregivers, or mental health professionals to meet their daily needs and maintain overall well-being.

Social Isolation and Stigma

Social isolation is a common experience for individuals living with schizophrenia, often exacerbated by the stigma and discrimination associated with mental illness. Many people with schizophrenia report feeling misunderstood, marginalized, or excluded from society due to their condition. Stigma can manifest in various forms, including negative stereotypes, fear, and avoidance behavior.

The impact of stigma extends beyond interpersonal relationships to societal attitudes and policies surrounding mental health. Discrimination in employment, housing, and healthcare can further limit opportunities for individuals with schizophrenia and contribute to their social and economic marginalization. Addressing stigma requires collective efforts to promote education, awareness, and empathy toward mental illness.

Coping Strategies and Support Systems

Despite the challenges posed by schizophrenia, many individuals find ways to cope and thrive with appropriate support and resources. Developing effective coping strategies involves identifying triggers, managing symptoms, and building resilience in the face of adversity. This may include engaging in self-care activities, pursuing creative outlets, and seeking social support from peers, family members, and mental health professionals.

Support systems play a crucial role in the recovery process for individuals with schizophrenia. Peer support groups, community mental health services, and advocacy organizations can provide validation, encouragement, and practical assistance to those navigating the complexities of living with schizophrenia. Building a supportive network can foster a sense of belonging and empowerment, reducing feelings of isolation and alienation.

Holistic Approaches to Mental Health

Holistic approaches to mental health emphasize the interconnectedness of mind, body, and spirit in promoting overall well-being. For individuals with schizophrenia, holistic interventions may encompass a range of modalities, including mindfulness-based practices, exercise, nutrition, and complementary therapies. These approaches aim to address the diverse needs of individuals with schizophrenia and promote recovery on multiple levels.

Incorporating holistic principles into mental health care requires collaboration among diverse stakeholders, including individuals with lived experience, healthcare providers, researchers, and policymakers. By adopting a holistic perspective, we can move beyond symptom management to promote holistic healing and enhance the quality of life for individuals living with schizophrenia.

Conclusion

Living with schizophrenia is a journey marked by challenges, resilience, and hope. Despite the complexities of the disorder, individuals with schizophrenia possess inherent strengths and abilities that deserve recognition and support. By fostering understanding, empathy, and inclusivity, we can create a more compassionate and equitable society for all individuals affected by mental illness. Through collaborative efforts and holistic approaches to mental health, we can empower individuals with schizophrenia to live meaningful and fulfilling lives, realizing their potential and contributing to the fabric of our communities.

Chapter 8. Post-Traumatic Stress Disorder (PTSD)
Healing from Trauma and Moving Forward

Introduction

In the landscape of mental health, Post-Traumatic Stress Disorder (PTSD) stands as a complex and often debilitating condition. It is a response to experiencing or witnessing traumatic events that overwhelm an individual's ability to cope. From combat veterans to survivors of abuse, natural disasters, or accidents, PTSD can affect anyone who has faced severe trauma. However, understanding and effectively addressing PTSD is crucial for individuals seeking to reclaim their lives and move forward.

Understanding PTSD

PTSD manifests in various ways, including intrusive memories, flashbacks, nightmares, hypervigilance, and emotional numbness. These symptoms can significantly impact an individual's daily functioning, relationships, and overall quality of life. Understanding the nature of PTSD involves recognizing that it's not a sign of weakness but a natural response to overwhelming events that shatter one's sense of safety and security.

The Neurobiology of Trauma

Research in neuroscience sheds light on the neurobiological underpinnings of PTSD. Traumatic experiences can dysregulate the brain's stress response system, particularly the amygdala and hippocampus, leading to heightened arousal and emotional reactivity. Moreover, alterations in neurotransmitter systems, such as serotonin and dopamine, contribute to mood disturbances and difficulties in regulating emotions commonly observed in individuals with PTSD.

Healing Trauma Holistically

Healing from PTSD necessitates a holistic approach that addresses the interconnectedness of the mind, body, and spirit. While traditional therapeutic interventions like cognitive-behavioral therapy (CBT) and Eye Movement Desensitization and Reprocessing (EMDR) are effective, integrating complementary modalities such as mindfulness, yoga, art therapy, and acupuncture can augment the healing process.

Cultivating Mindfulness

Mindfulness practices cultivate present-moment awareness and non-judgmental acceptance of one's experiences. By learning to observe thoughts and emotions without becoming entangled in them, individuals with PTSD can develop greater emotional regulation and resilience. Mindfulness-based interventions, such as Mindfulness-Based Stress Reduction (MBSR) and Mindfulness-Based Cognitive Therapy (MBCT), have demonstrated efficacy in reducing PTSD symptoms and improving overall well-being.

Mindfulness-Based Stress Reduction (MBSR): An evidence-based program developed by Jon Kabat-Zinn that combines mindfulness meditation and yoga techniques to help individuals reduce stress, manage pain, and improve overall well-being. MBSR teaches participants to cultivate present-moment awareness, non-judgmental observation of thoughts and emotions, and acceptance of experiences as they arise.

Mindfulness-Based Cognitive Therapy (MBCT): A therapeutic approach that integrates principles of cognitive therapy with mindfulness practices to prevent relapse in individuals with recurrent depression. MBCT helps individuals become more aware of negative thought patterns and teaches skills to disengage from automatic reactivity, reduce rumination, and cultivate a compassionate and accepting attitude toward oneself.

Embodied Healing through Yoga

Yoga offers a somatic approach to healing trauma by integrating movement, breathwork, and mindfulness practices. Through gentle asanas (poses) and pranayama (breathing techniques), individuals can release stored tension and promote relaxation within the body. Yoga also fosters a sense of empowerment and agency, allowing individuals to reconnect with their bodies in a safe and supportive environment, which is often disrupted by trauma.

Art Therapy and Expressive Arts

Art therapy provides a creative outlet for processing emotions and experiences that may be difficult to verbalize. Through various artistic mediums such as painting, drawing, sculpting, and writing, individuals can externalize their internal worlds, gain insights, and foster self-expression. Engaging in the creative process can promote catharsis, meaning-making, and the exploration of new narratives beyond the confines of trauma.

Acupuncture and Traditional Chinese Medicine (TCM)

Acupuncture, an integral component of Traditional Chinese Medicine (TCM), operates on the principle of restoring balance and harmony within the body's energy systems, known as Qi. By stimulating specific acupoints along meridian pathways, acupuncture can alleviate symptoms of anxiety, depression, and PTSD. Moreover, TCM modalities such as herbal medicine and Qigong (energy cultivation exercises) complement acupuncture in addressing underlying imbalances contributing to PTSD.

Building Resilience and Social Support

Recovery from PTSD is not a solitary journey but one that thrives on connections and support networks. Building resilience involves nurturing meaningful relationships, fostering a sense of belonging, and seeking support from peers, family, and mental health professionals. Group therapy and peer support programs offer opportunities for individuals with PTSD to share experiences, gain perspective, and cultivate a sense of community grounded in empathy and understanding.

Honoring the Journey of Healing

Healing from PTSD is a nonlinear process characterized by ups and downs, setbacks, and breakthroughs. It requires patience, self-compassion, and a willingness to confront challenges with courage and resilience. While the path to recovery may be arduous, every step taken towards healing is a testament to the innate human capacity for transformation and growth.

Conclusion

Post-Traumatic Stress Disorder (PTSD) represents a profound disruption of the self in the aftermath of trauma. However, healing is not only possible but achievable through a multifaceted approach that addresses the holistic needs of individuals affected by PTSD. By integrating therapeutic modalities that encompass the mind, body, and spirit, individuals can embark on a journey of healing, reclaiming their lives, and moving forward with hope and resilience. As we continue to deepen our understanding of PTSD and refine our approaches to treatment, let us uphold a compassionate and inclusive vision of mental health that honors the inherent dignity and worth of every individual on their path to healing.

Chapter 9. Obsessive-Compulsive Disorder (OCD)
Exploring the Cycle of Intrusive Thoughts and Compulsions

Introduction

Obsessive-Compulsive Disorder (OCD) is a mental health condition characterized by persistent, intrusive thoughts (obsessions) and repetitive behaviors or mental acts (compulsions) aimed at reducing the anxiety associated with these obsessions. It affects people of all ages, genders, and backgrounds, causing significant distress and interference in daily life. Understanding the cycle of intrusive thoughts and compulsions is crucial for effective management and treatment of OCD.

Understanding Obsessions

Obsessions are intrusive, distressing thoughts, images, or urges that repeatedly enter an individual's mind, causing intense anxiety or discomfort. These thoughts often center around themes such as contamination, symmetry, orderliness, harm, or unacceptable/taboo subjects. Individuals with OCD may recognize these obsessions as irrational, but they struggle to control or dismiss them.

The Role of Compulsions

Compulsions are repetitive behaviors or mental acts that individuals with OCD feel driven to perform in response to their obsessions. These actions are aimed at reducing distress or preventing a feared event, although they provide only temporary relief. Common compulsions include washing, checking, counting, repeating words or phrases, and arranging objects in a specific way.

The Cycle of Obsessions and Compulsions

The cycle of OCD typically begins with the onset of intrusive thoughts or images (obsessions), which trigger intense anxiety, fear, or discomfort. In an attempt to alleviate this distress, individuals engage in compulsive behaviors or mental rituals (compulsions). While these compulsions may temporarily reduce anxiety, they reinforce the belief that the obsessions are significant and warrant attention.

Reinforcement and Escalation

The temporary relief provided by compulsions reinforces the cycle of OCD, leading to a pattern of escalating obsessions and compulsions over time. Individuals may find themselves trapped in a cycle of increasing distress and preoccupation with their symptoms, which can significantly impair their quality of life and functioning.

The Vicious Cycle of Avoidance

In addition to engaging in compulsions, individuals with OCD often resort to avoidance behaviors to prevent triggering their obsessions. For example, someone with contamination obsessions may avoid public places or refuse to touch certain objects. While avoidance may provide temporary relief, it reinforces the belief that the feared outcome is likely to occur, perpetuating the cycle of OCD.

The Impact on Daily Life

OCD can have a profound impact on various aspects of daily life, including work, school, relationships, and overall well-being. The time-consuming nature of obsessions and compulsions can interfere with productivity and social interactions, leading to feelings of isolation, frustration, and shame. Many individuals with OCD experience significant impairment in their ability to function effectively in different domains of life.

The Interplay of Genetics, Environment, and Neurobiology

The exact causes of OCD are not fully understood, but research suggests that a combination of genetic, environmental, and neurobiological factors may contribute to its development. Certain genetic predispositions, along with environmental stressors and abnormalities in brain chemistry, may increase the risk of developing OCD. However, the precise mechanisms underlying the disorder require further investigation.

Treatment Approaches for OCD

Effective treatment for OCD typically involves a combination of medication, psychotherapy, and lifestyle modifications. Selective serotonin reuptake inhibitors (SSRIs) are commonly prescribed to alleviate symptoms by regulating neurotransmitter levels in the brain. Cognitive-behavioral therapy (CBT), particularly exposure and response prevention (ERP), is highly effective in helping individuals confront and manage their obsessions and compulsions.

Exposure and Response Prevention (ERP) is a cognitive-behavioral therapy technique primarily used to treat obsessive-compulsive disorder (OCD) and other anxiety disorders. ERP involves exposing individuals to anxiety-provoking stimuli or situations (exposure) while preventing them from engaging in compulsive or avoidant behaviors (response prevention). Through repeated exposure to feared stimuli without engaging in compulsions, individuals gradually learn that their feared outcomes are unlikely to occur, leading to a reduction in anxiety and the weakening of obsessive-compulsive patterns. ERP aims to help individuals develop more adaptive coping mechanisms and reduce the impact of anxiety on their daily functioning.

Mindfulness and Acceptance-Based Therapies

Mindfulness-based approaches, such as mindfulness-based cognitive therapy (MBCT) and acceptance and commitment therapy (ACT), can also be beneficial for individuals with OCD. These therapies focus on developing acceptance of intrusive thoughts without engaging in compulsive behaviors, helping individuals cultivate greater psychological flexibility and resilience in the face of uncertainty.

Acceptance and Commitment Therapy (ACT) is a form of psychotherapy that combines mindfulness techniques with strategies for increasing psychological flexibility and fostering values-based action. ACT aims to help individuals develop psychological skills to effectively handle difficult thoughts and feelings while pursuing a meaningful and fulfilling life. Key components of ACT include acceptance of present moment experiences, cognitive defusion (creating distance from one's thoughts), being present and mindful, clarifying personal values, and taking committed action towards values-based goals. ACT is used to treat various psychological issues, including anxiety, depression, chronic pain, substance abuse, and other mental health conditions.

The Importance of Self-Care and Support

In addition to professional treatment, self-care practices and social support play a crucial role in managing OCD. Engaging in regular exercise, maintaining a balanced diet, practicing relaxation techniques, and prioritizing adequate sleep can help reduce stress and improve overall well-being. Building a strong support network of family, friends, and support groups can provide encouragement, understanding, and validation during the recovery process.

Challenging Stigma and Misconceptions

Stigma and misconceptions surrounding OCD can further exacerbate the challenges faced by individuals living with the disorder. It is essential to challenge stereotypes and promote awareness and understanding of OCD as a legitimate mental health condition. Education, advocacy, and open dialogue can help reduce stigma and encourage individuals to seek help and support without fear of judgment or discrimination.

Promoting Holistic Well-Being

Taking a holistic approach to mental health involves addressing the interconnected aspects of physical, emotional, and social well-being. For individuals living with OCD, this may involve integrating various strategies and interventions to manage symptoms while fostering resilience and self-compassion. By prioritizing holistic well-being, individuals can cultivate a sense of empowerment and agency in their journey toward recovery.

Conclusion

Obsessive-Compulsive Disorder (OCD) is a complex mental health condition characterized by the cycle of intrusive thoughts and compulsions. Understanding this cycle is crucial for effective management and treatment of OCD, which often involves a combination of medication, therapy, self-care, and social support. By challenging stigma, promoting awareness, and embracing holistic approaches to well-being, individuals with OCD can embark on a path of healing and empowerment. It is essential to foster a compassionate and supportive environment where individuals feel empowered to seek help and live fulfilling lives beyond the confines of their symptoms.

Introduction

Understanding mental health involves delving into the intricate interplay between genetics and the environment. Both factors significantly contribute to an individual's psychological well-being, shaping the way they perceive, think, and react to the world around them. This holistic approach to mental health acknowledges the complex interaction between genetic predispositions and environmental influences. In this article, we explore the nuanced relationship between genetics and environment and their impact on mental health outcomes.

Genetics

Genetics forms the foundation of mental health, influencing the risk of developing various psychiatric disorders. The intricate network of genes inherited from parents serves as the blueprint for an individual's physiological and psychological traits. Research in the field of behavioral genetics has identified numerous genetic factors associated with mental health disorders, including schizophrenia, bipolar disorder, depression, and anxiety disorders.

The Role of Genetic Variations

Genetic variations, such as single nucleotide polymorphisms (SNPs) and copy number variations (CNVs), contribute to the susceptibility to mental health disorders. These variations may alter the structure and function of key neurotransmitter systems, synaptic connectivity, and neural circuits implicated in emotional regulation and cognitive processing. For instance, variations in genes encoding serotonin transporters and receptors have been linked to the development of depression and anxiety disorders.

Understanding Gene-Environment Interplay

However, genetics alone does not determine mental health outcomes. The interplay between genetic predispositions and environmental influences plays a crucial role in shaping individual vulnerabilities to psychiatric disorders. The diathesis-stress model proposes that genetic predispositions interact with environmental stressors to trigger the onset of mental illness. Thus, individuals with genetic vulnerabilities may be more susceptible to the adverse effects of environmental stressors, such as trauma, abuse, or chronic stress.

Environmental Factors

Environmental factors encompass a broad spectrum of influences, ranging from early life experiences and social interactions to socioeconomic status and access to healthcare services. These environmental exposures significantly impact brain development, emotional regulation, and cognitive functioning, thereby shaping mental health outcomes across the lifespan.

Early Life Experiences

Early life experiences, including prenatal factors, maternal stress, and childhood adversity, profoundly influence neurodevelopment and susceptibility to mental health disorders later in life. Adverse childhood experiences, such as neglect, abuse, or parental psychopathology, increase the risk of developing mood disorders, post-traumatic stress disorder (PTSD), and substance abuse disorders. Moreover, prenatal exposure to maternal stress, substance abuse, or environmental toxins can disrupt fetal neurodevelopment, predisposing offspring to psychiatric vulnerabilities.

Social Determinants of Mental Health

Social determinants, including socioeconomic status, education, employment, and social support networks, shape the psychosocial context in which individuals experience mental health challenges. Socioeconomic disparities exacerbate stressors and limit access to mental healthcare resources, perpetuating inequalities in mental health outcomes among marginalized populations. Moreover, social isolation, discrimination, and stigma contribute to the burden of mental illness and hinder help-seeking behaviors among affected individuals.

Lifestyle Factors and Mental Well-being

Lifestyle choices, such as diet, physical activity, sleep patterns, and substance use, profoundly impact mental well-being. A healthy lifestyle that prioritizes nutrition, regular exercise, adequate sleep, and stress management can enhance resilience against mental health challenges and promote overall psychological wellness. Conversely, unhealthy behaviors, such as sedentary lifestyle, poor dietary habits, substance abuse, and sleep deprivation, increase the risk of developing mood disorders, anxiety, and cognitive impairments.

Epigenetics

Epigenetics is the study of heritable changes in gene expression and function that occur without alterations to the underlying DNA sequence, influenced by environmental factors and lifestyle choices. Epigenetics serves as the interface between genetics and the environment, modulating gene expression in response to environmental cues. Epigenetic mechanisms, including DNA methylation, histone modifications, and non-coding RNAs, regulate gene activity and cellular responses to environmental stimuli. Environmental exposures, such as diet, stress, trauma, and environmental toxins, can induce epigenetic changes that alter neural plasticity, stress reactivity, and susceptibility to mental health disorders.

Transgenerational Effects of Environmental Exposures

Emerging evidence suggests that environmental exposures experienced across generations can influence the epigenetic programming of offspring, contributing to transgenerational inheritance of psychiatric vulnerabilities. Prenatal and early-life exposures to maternal stress, trauma, or environmental toxins can induce epigenetic modifications that persist across generations, predisposing offspring to mental health disorders later in life. These transgenerational effects underscore the importance of early intervention and preventive strategies to break the cycle of intergenerational transmission of mental illness.

Conclusion

Mental health is shaped by a complex interplay between genetic predispositions and environmental influences. Genetics provides the foundation for individual vulnerabilities to psychiatric disorders, while environmental factors modulate gene expression and neural circuitry, shaping mental health outcomes across the lifespan. Recognizing the synergistic relationship between genetics and environment is essential for developing holistic approaches to mental health promotion, prevention, and intervention. By addressing genetic predispositions, mitigating environmental stressors, and fostering supportive environments, we can enhance resilience and promote mental well-being for individuals and communities alike.

Introduction

In recent years, there has been a growing recognition of the importance of mental health in children and adolescents. The early years of life lay the foundation for emotional well-being and resilience, making childhood and adolescence critical periods for intervention and support. Addressing mental health issues during these formative years not only improves immediate outcomes but also contributes to long-term positive development. In this article, we will explore the significance of early intervention and support in childhood and adolescent mental health.

Understanding Childhood and Adolescent Mental Health

Childhood and adolescence are characterized by rapid physical, cognitive, and emotional growth. During these stages, children and teenagers encounter various challenges that can impact their mental health. These challenges may include academic stress, peer pressure, family dynamics, and societal expectations. Additionally, biological factors, genetic predispositions, and early life experiences play significant roles in shaping mental health outcomes.

Early Signs and Symptoms

Recognizing the signs and symptoms of mental health issues in children and adolescents is crucial for early intervention. While the manifestations of mental health problems can vary widely, common indicators may include changes in behavior, mood swings, social withdrawal, academic decline, irritability, and physical complaints without medical cause. Parents, caregivers, teachers, and healthcare professionals play vital roles in observing and identifying these signs.

The Importance of Early Intervention

Early intervention in childhood and adolescence offers several advantages. Firstly, it allows for timely support and treatment, reducing the risk of long-term complications. Early intervention strategies can help prevent the escalation of mental health problems and mitigate their impact on various aspects of a child's life, including academic performance, social relationships, and self-esteem. Moreover, addressing mental health issues early can promote resilience and adaptive coping skills, empowering children and adolescents to navigate challenges effectively.

Building Supportive Environments

Creating supportive environments is essential for promoting mental health and well-being in children and adolescents. Supportive environments encompass family dynamics, school settings, peer relationships, and community resources. Families play a central role in providing emotional support, nurturing positive relationships, and fostering open communication about mental health issues. Schools can implement programs that promote mental health literacy, resilience-building, and access to counseling services. Peer support networks and community organizations offer additional avenues for social connection and support.

Access to Mental Health Services

Access to mental health services remains a critical factor in early intervention and support. Unfortunately, many children and adolescents face barriers to accessing appropriate care, including stigma, financial constraints, and limited availability of services. Efforts to improve access to mental health services should address these barriers through advocacy, policy reforms, and the integration of mental health into primary care settings. Telehealth platforms and digital interventions also hold promise for expanding access to mental health support, particularly in underserved communities.

Preventive Strategies

In addition to early intervention, preventive strategies play a vital role in promoting childhood and adolescent mental health. Prevention efforts focus on addressing risk factors, promoting protective factors, and fostering resilience across various domains. Targeted interventions may include parent education programs, school-based mental health initiatives, psychoeducation campaigns, and community outreach efforts. By addressing risk factors such as adverse childhood experiences, trauma, and substance abuse, preventive strategies aim to mitigate the onset and progression of mental health problems.

The Role of Resilience

Resilience is a key factor in promoting mental health and well-being in children and adolescents. Resilience encompasses the ability to adapt to adversity, bounce back from setbacks, and thrive in the face of challenges. Building resilience involves developing coping skills, fostering positive relationships, nurturing a sense of self-efficacy, and promoting problem-solving abilities. Resilience-oriented interventions aim to strengthen protective factors and enhance children's ability to cope with stressors effectively.

Family Dynamics and Support

Family dynamics play a central role in shaping children's mental health outcomes. Positive family relationships, secure attachments, and effective communication contribute to emotional stability and psychological well-being. Conversely, dysfunctional family dynamics, parental conflict, and adverse childhood experiences can increase the risk of mental health problems. Family-based interventions focus on improving communication patterns, resolving conflicts, and providing parents with the skills and support they need to nurture their children's mental health.

Cultural Considerations

Cultural factors influence perceptions of mental health, help-seeking behaviors, and treatment preferences among children and adolescents. Cultural beliefs, values, and traditions shape individuals' understanding of mental illness and influence their attitudes toward seeking professional help. It is essential for mental health professionals to recognize and respect cultural diversity in their practice, tailoring interventions to meet the unique needs of diverse populations. Culturally sensitive approaches foster trust, enhance engagement, and improve treatment outcomes.

Educational Support and Advocacy

Educational institutions play a crucial role in supporting the mental health needs of children and adolescents. Schools can implement policies that promote mental health awareness, reduce stigma, and facilitate early identification of mental health concerns. Educators and school counselors play pivotal roles in providing emotional support, crisis intervention, and referrals to mental health services. Advocacy efforts aimed at increasing funding for school-based mental health programs and improving access to counseling services are essential for creating mentally healthy school environments.

Conclusion

Childhood and adolescence represent critical periods for promoting mental health and well-being. Early intervention and support are essential components of a holistic approach to mental health care for children and adolescents. By recognizing early signs and symptoms, building supportive environments, improving access to mental health services, implementing preventive strategies, fostering resilience, addressing family dynamics, considering cultural factors, and advocating for educational support, we can empower children and adolescents to thrive emotionally and psychologically. Investing in the mental health of young people today yields dividends in their future well-being and quality of life.

Introduction

In today's fast-paced world, the challenges to adult mental health have become increasingly prevalent. Stress, anxiety, and depression are among the most common mental health issues affecting adults worldwide. Coping with these challenges requires a multifaceted approach that addresses both the external stressors and internal struggles individuals face. This article delves into the complexities of adult mental health, exploring strategies for coping with stress, anxiety, and depression in a holistic manner.

Understanding Stress

Stress is an inevitable part of life, but chronic stress can take a toll on mental and physical well-being. In the modern world, adults often juggle multiple responsibilities, such as work, family, and social obligations, leading to heightened stress levels. Recognizing the signs of stress is the first step in coping effectively. Symptoms may manifest as irritability, fatigue, insomnia, and difficulty concentrating. It's essential to identify stressors and develop healthy coping mechanisms to manage them.

Coping Strategies for Stress

Effective stress management involves adopting healthy lifestyle habits and prioritizing self-care. Engaging in regular physical activity, such as exercise or yoga, can help reduce stress levels by promoting the release of endorphins, the body's natural stress relievers. Additionally, practicing relaxation techniques, such as deep breathing exercises or mindfulness meditation, can calm the mind and promote a sense of inner peace. Creating boundaries and learning to say no to excessive demands can also alleviate stress and prevent burnout.

Understanding Anxiety

Anxiety disorders are among the most common mental health conditions, affecting millions of adults worldwide. Unlike occasional feelings of nervousness or worry, anxiety disorders involve persistent and excessive fear or apprehension that interferes with daily functioning. Generalized anxiety disorder (GAD), panic disorder, social anxiety disorder, and phobias are some common forms of anxiety disorders. Understanding the underlying causes and triggers of anxiety is crucial for developing effective coping strategies.

Coping Strategies for Anxiety

Managing anxiety often requires a combination of therapeutic interventions and lifestyle modifications. Cognitive-behavioral therapy (CBT) is a widely used therapeutic approach that helps individuals identify and challenge negative thought patterns associated with anxiety. Learning relaxation techniques, such as progressive muscle relaxation or visualization exercises, can help reduce anxiety symptoms and promote a sense of calmness. Building a strong support network and seeking professional help when needed are essential steps in managing anxiety effectively.

Understanding Depression

Depression is a serious mood disorder characterized by persistent feelings of sadness, hopelessness, and loss of interest in activities once enjoyed. It can significantly impact one's quality of life and impair functioning in various areas, including work, relationships, and daily activities. While everyone experiences feelings of sadness from time to time, depression is more than just occasional blues - it's a debilitating condition that requires timely intervention and support.

Coping Strategies for Depression

Treating depression often involves a combination of therapy, medication, and lifestyle changes. Cognitive-behavioral therapy (CBT) and interpersonal therapy (IPT) are commonly used psychotherapeutic approaches for treating depression by addressing negative thought patterns and improving interpersonal relationships. Antidepressant medications, such as selective serotonin reuptake inhibitors (SSRIs) or serotonin-norepinephrine reuptake inhibitors (SNRIs), may be prescribed in conjunction with therapy to alleviate symptoms. Engaging in activities that bring joy and purpose, maintaining a healthy sleep schedule, and seeking social support are vital components of depression management.

Holistic Approach to Mental Health

Taking a holistic approach to mental health involves addressing the interconnectedness of the mind, body, and spirit. It encompasses nurturing physical health through proper nutrition, regular exercise, and adequate sleep. It also involves fostering emotional well-being through mindfulness practices, stress management techniques, and therapeutic interventions. Additionally, connecting with others, cultivating meaningful relationships, and finding purpose and fulfillment in life contribute to overall mental health and resilience.

Building Resilience

Resilience is the ability to bounce back from adversity and adapt to life's challenges with strength and flexibility. Developing resilience involves cultivating self-awareness, fostering positive coping strategies, and nurturing supportive relationships. It's about learning from setbacks, maintaining a hopeful outlook, and embracing change as an opportunity for growth. Building resilience is an ongoing process that requires patience, perseverance, and self-compassion.

Conclusion

Adult mental health challenges, such as stress, anxiety, and depression, are pervasive issues that require proactive management and support. By understanding the underlying causes and implementing holistic coping strategies, individuals can cultivate resilience and enhance their overall well-being. From practicing self-care and seeking professional help to nurturing meaningful connections and embracing life's ups and downs, there are myriad ways to cope with mental health challenges and thrive in today's complex world. Remember, reaching out for support is a sign of strength, and no one has to face mental health struggles alone.

Introduction

In the intricate tapestry of mental health, relationships and communication serve as crucial threads that can either strengthen or unravel the fabric of well-being. The dynamics of our relationships, be they romantic, familial, or platonic, often mirror the state of our mental health. Understanding how to navigate these relationships with empathy, honesty, and effective communication can significantly impact our psychological well-being. In this comprehensive guide, we delve into the intricate interplay between relationships and mental health, exploring the importance of support systems and communication in fostering resilience and emotional wellness.

Understanding the Interconnection

Relationships and mental health share a symbiotic relationship, each influencing the other in profound ways. Our mental well-being shapes how we perceive and engage in relationships, while the quality of our relationships can either nurture or challenge our mental health. For instance, individuals struggling with mental health issues such as depression or anxiety may find it challenging to maintain healthy relationships due to emotional fluctuations and social withdrawal. Conversely, supportive and nurturing relationships can serve as a buffer against stressors and contribute to psychological resilience.

Building Support Systems

At the heart of navigating relationships and mental health lies the concept of support systems. These networks encompass individuals, communities, and resources that provide emotional validation, practical assistance, and unconditional acceptance during times of distress. Support systems can include family members, friends, mental health professionals, support groups, and online communities. Cultivating a diverse support network is essential, as different individuals may offer unique perspectives and forms of support.

Family Dynamics and Mental Health

Family relationships exert a profound influence on our mental well-being, shaping our sense of identity, belonging, and emotional stability. Healthy family dynamics are characterized by open communication, mutual respect, and unconditional love. However, family conflicts, dysfunction, or trauma can significantly impact mental health, leading to feelings of alienation, anxiety, or depression. Recognizing and addressing familial issues through therapy, mediation, or boundary-setting is crucial for fostering emotional healing and restoring relational harmony.

Romantic Relationships

Romantic relationships represent a complex interplay of emotions, desires, and expectations, with profound implications for mental health. Healthy romantic partnerships are built on a foundation of trust, intimacy, and effective communication. Couples who prioritize emotional attunement, active listening, and conflict resolution strategies are better equipped to navigate the inevitable challenges and stressors that arise. Setting boundaries, honoring individual autonomy, and fostering mutual support are essential components of a thriving romantic relationship.

Friendship and Social Support

Friendships serve as vital pillars of support in navigating life's challenges and triumphs. Close friendships offer companionship, laughter, and a sense of belonging that can bolster mental resilience and provide solace during difficult times. Cultivating authentic connections based on mutual trust, empathy, and shared interests is key to nurturing meaningful friendships. Social support networks, both online and offline, provide avenues for validation, empathy, and practical assistance, fostering a sense of community and belonging.

Effective Communication

Central to the fabric of healthy relationships is effective communication - the cornerstone of emotional intimacy, trust, and mutual understanding. Effective communication involves not only expressing one's thoughts and feelings but also actively listening with empathy and non-judgment. Honesty, transparency, and vulnerability form the bedrock of authentic communication, fostering deeper connections and emotional intimacy. Learning to communicate assertively, set boundaries, and resolve conflicts constructively are essential skills for maintaining healthy relationships.

Navigating Challenges and Seeking Help

Despite our best efforts, relationships inevitably encounter challenges and conflicts that can strain our mental health. External stressors, life transitions, and individual differences may contribute to tension and discord within relationships. During such times, seeking professional guidance from therapists, counselors, or relationship experts can provide invaluable support and perspective. Therapy offers a safe space to explore relational dynamics, enhance communication skills, and address underlying issues contributing to distress.

Cultivating Self-Compassion and Resilience

In navigating relationships and mental health, cultivating self-compassion and resilience is paramount. Self-compassion involves treating oneself with kindness, acceptance, and understanding, especially during times of vulnerability or self-doubt. Embracing one's imperfections, practicing self-care, and setting realistic expectations are essential components of self-compassionate living. Resilience, the ability to bounce back from adversity, is nurtured through meaningful connections, adaptive coping strategies, and a sense of purpose and meaning in life.

Conclusion

In the tapestry of human experience, relationships and mental health are intricately woven together, shaping our sense of identity, belonging, and emotional well-being. Navigating relationships with empathy, authenticity, and effective communication is essential for fostering resilience, emotional intimacy, and relational harmony. Building robust support systems, cultivating self-compassion, and seeking professional guidance when needed are vital steps in promoting mental wellness and nurturing thriving relationships. By honoring the interconnection between relationships and mental health, we pave the way for deeper connections, emotional healing, and collective flourishing.

Introduction

Mental health issues have gained significant attention in recent years as societies worldwide grapple with the complexities of psychological well-being. In the pursuit of holistic mental health care, psychotherapy and counseling emerge as pivotal therapeutic approaches. These methodologies encompass a range of techniques and theories aimed at addressing diverse mental health concerns. This article delves into the essence of psychotherapy and counseling, exploring their principles, methodologies, and their roles in promoting mental wellness.

Understanding Psychotherapy

Psychotherapy, often interchangeably referred to as talk therapy, encompasses a broad spectrum of therapeutic interventions aimed at improving an individual's mental health and well-being. Rooted in psychological principles, psychotherapy facilitates understanding and managing emotions, behaviors, and thoughts. One of the fundamental aspects of psychotherapy is the therapeutic relationship between the therapist and the client, fostering trust, empathy, and collaboration.

Types of Psychotherapy

1. Cognitive-Behavioral Therapy (CBT)

CBT is a widely utilized form of psychotherapy that focuses on identifying and modifying negative thought patterns and behaviors. Through cognitive restructuring and behavior modification techniques, individuals learn to challenge and replace maladaptive beliefs, leading to improved emotional regulation and coping strategies.

2. Psychodynamic Therapy

Psychodynamic therapy delves into the unconscious mind, exploring how past experiences and unresolved conflicts influence present behavior and emotions. Through self-exploration and insight, clients gain a deeper understanding of their inner workings, paving the way for personal growth and healing.

3. Humanistic Therapy

Humanistic therapy emphasizes self-awareness, personal responsibility, and the pursuit of self-actualization. With an emphasis on empathy, authenticity, and unconditional positive regard, humanistic therapists create a supportive environment where clients can explore their feelings, values, and potentialities freely.

4. Existential Therapy

Existential therapy delves into the existential concerns of human existence, such as freedom, meaning, and mortality. By confronting existential anxieties and embracing life's uncertainties, individuals can cultivate a sense of purpose and authenticity, fostering psychological resilience and fulfillment.

Counseling: A Collaborative Journey

Counseling shares similarities with psychotherapy but often focuses on specific issues or life transitions, offering guidance, support, and practical solutions to clients facing challenges. While psychotherapy tends to explore deep-seated emotional issues, counseling tends to be more problem-focused and goal-oriented, addressing immediate concerns and facilitating positive changes.

Types of Counseling

1. Marriage and Family Counseling

Marriage and family counselors work with couples and families to improve communication, resolve conflicts, and strengthen relationships. By fostering understanding and empathy, counselors help families navigate challenges and build healthier dynamics.

2. Career Counseling

Career counselors assist individuals in exploring career options, identifying strengths and interests, and overcoming obstacles in their professional lives. Through assessments, goal-setting, and skill development, clients can make informed decisions and pursue fulfilling career paths.

3. Substance Abuse Counseling

Substance abuse counselors specialize in helping individuals overcome addiction and substance dependency. By providing support, education, and therapeutic interventions, counselors empower clients to break free from destructive patterns and achieve sobriety.

The Therapeutic Process

Regardless of the specific approach, the therapeutic process typically unfolds in several stages, each contributing to the client's growth and healing.

1. Assessment and Evaluation

The therapist conducts an initial assessment to gain insight into the client's presenting concerns, personal history, and treatment goals. Through interviews, questionnaires, and standardized assessments, therapists gather information to inform the therapeutic approach.

2. Goal Setting

Collaboratively, the therapist and client establish clear and achievable goals that guide the therapeutic journey. These goals serve as benchmarks for progress and provide direction for the treatment process.

3. Intervention and Techniques

Drawing from theoretical frameworks and evidence-based practices, therapists employ various interventions and techniques tailored to the client's needs and preferences. These may include cognitive restructuring, relaxation techniques, role-playing, journaling, and mindfulness exercises, among others.

Cognitive restructuring: Reframing negative thoughts to promote healthier perspectives and beliefs.

Relaxation techniques: Utilizing methods like deep breathing, progressive muscle relaxation, and visualization to reduce stress and induce calmness.

Role-playing: Actively assuming different perspectives or roles to understand situations and relationships better.

Journaling: Writing thoughts, feelings, and experiences to gain insight, process emotions, and track personal growth.

Mindfulness exercises: Engaging in present-moment awareness practices to cultivate attention, acceptance, and non-judgmental awareness of thoughts, emotions, and sensations.

4. Reflection and Integration

Throughout the therapeutic process, clients are encouraged to reflect on their experiences, insights, and progress. By integrating newfound awareness and coping strategies into their daily lives, clients can effect positive change and sustain long-term well-being.

The Role of the Therapist

Therapists play a multifaceted role in the therapeutic process, serving as guides, facilitators, and advocates for their clients' mental health and wellness. Key attributes of effective therapists include empathy, active listening, cultural competence, and a commitment to ongoing professional development.

Challenges and Considerations

While psychotherapy and counseling offer invaluable support and resources for individuals grappling with mental health concerns, several challenges and considerations merit attention.

1. Accessibility and Affordability

Access to quality mental health care remains a significant barrier for many individuals, particularly those from marginalized communities or low-income backgrounds. Addressing disparities in access and affordability is crucial for ensuring equitable mental health services for all.

2. Stigma and Cultural Factors

Stigma surrounding mental illness and cultural beliefs about therapy can deter individuals from seeking help or adhering to treatment recommendations. Culturally sensitive approaches that honor diverse perspectives and experiences are essential for fostering trust and engagement in therapy.

3. Integration of Technology

The advent of teletherapy and digital mental health platforms has expanded access to therapy and counseling services, particularly in remote or underserved areas. However, ethical considerations regarding data privacy, security, and the quality of online interventions remain paramount.

Conclusion

Psychotherapy and counseling stand as cornerstone approaches in the holistic care of mental health, offering individuals a pathway to healing, growth, and resilience. By fostering self-awareness, empowerment, and connection, these therapeutic modalities empower individuals to navigate life's challenges with greater clarity, purpose, and well-being. As we continue to advance our understanding of mental health and wellness, integrating diverse approaches and promoting accessibility and inclusivity remain imperative for fostering thriving communities and individuals.

Introduction

In the realm of mental health treatment, medications play a significant role in managing symptoms and improving the quality of life for individuals facing various mental health challenges. However, the decision to use medications is not a one-size-fits-all approach. It involves a delicate balance between the potential benefits they offer and the risks they pose. Understanding the complexities surrounding medication use in mental health care is crucial for both patients and healthcare providers. This article delves into the nuances of medication management, exploring the benefits, risks, and considerations involved in finding the right balance for optimal mental health treatment.

The Role of Medications in Mental Health Treatment

Medications for mental health conditions, such as antidepressants, antipsychotics, mood stabilizers, and anxiolytics, are designed to alleviate symptoms and help individuals regain stability in their daily lives. They work by targeting neurotransmitters in the brain, restoring chemical imbalances, and regulating mood, cognition, and behavior. For many individuals, medications serve as a vital component of their treatment plan, offering relief from debilitating symptoms and facilitating recovery.

Benefits of Medications in Mental Health Treatment

One of the primary benefits of medications is their ability to provide rapid relief from acute symptoms. In cases of severe depression, anxiety, or psychosis, medications can offer timely intervention, helping individuals regain their emotional equilibrium and prevent further deterioration of mental health. Moreover, medications can enhance the effectiveness of psychotherapy by reducing symptoms that may impede the therapeutic process. By alleviating distressing symptoms, medications enable individuals to engage more fully in therapy, explore underlying issues, and develop coping strategies for long-term recovery.

Another significant benefit of medications is their role in preventing relapse and recurrence of mental health symptoms. For individuals with chronic conditions like bipolar disorder or schizophrenia, maintenance medications help stabilize mood and reduce the frequency and severity of episodes. By adhering to a prescribed medication regimen, individuals can better manage their symptoms, maintain stability, and prevent debilitating relapses that may disrupt their lives and relationships.

Furthermore, medications can improve overall functioning and quality of life for individuals with mental health conditions. By alleviating symptoms such as low energy, poor concentration, and impaired social functioning, medications enable individuals to participate more fully in work, school, and social activities. This restoration of functioning enhances self-esteem, promotes independence, and fosters a sense of well-being, empowering individuals to lead fulfilling lives despite the challenges posed by their mental health condition.

Risks and Challenges Associated with Medications

While medications offer substantial benefits, they are not without risks and challenges. Like any medical intervention, psychiatric medications can have side effects ranging from mild discomfort to severe complications.

Common side effects may include drowsiness, weight gain, sexual dysfunction, gastrointestinal disturbances, and cognitive impairment. For some individuals, these side effects can be tolerable and transient, diminishing over time as the body adjusts to the medication. However, for others, side effects may be intolerable, leading to non-compliance with treatment or the need for additional interventions to manage symptoms.

Moreover, psychiatric medications carry the risk of adverse reactions and complications, particularly when used in combination with other medications or in individuals with pre-existing medical conditions. Drug interactions, allergic reactions, and paradoxical effects are potential concerns that require careful monitoring and oversight by healthcare providers. Additionally, some medications may pose a risk of dependency or withdrawal symptoms, especially if discontinued abruptly or used in high doses over an extended period.

Another challenge associated with medications is the trial-and-error process involved in finding the most effective and tolerable treatment regimen for each individual. Since response to medications varies widely among patients, healthcare providers often need to experiment with different medications, dosages, and combinations to achieve optimal outcomes. This trial-and-error approach can be frustrating and time-consuming for both patients and providers, delaying symptom relief and impeding progress towards recovery.

Balancing Benefits and Risks

In navigating the complex terrain of medication management in mental health care, several key considerations emerge to guide treatment decisions and optimize outcomes. First and foremost, a collaborative and patient-centered approach is essential, emphasizing open communication, shared decision-making, and mutual respect between patients and healthcare providers. By actively involving patients in the treatment process, healthcare providers can gain valuable insights into their preferences, concerns, and treatment goals, fostering a sense of empowerment and autonomy in managing their mental health.

Secondly, comprehensive assessment and monitoring are paramount to ensure the safe and effective use of medications. Prior to initiating treatment, healthcare providers should conduct a thorough evaluation of the patient's medical history, psychiatric symptoms, co-occurring conditions, and medication preferences. Ongoing monitoring and regular follow-up appointments allow for the early detection of side effects, treatment response, and changes in clinical status, enabling timely adjustments to the treatment plan as needed.

Furthermore, education and psychoeducation play a crucial role in empowering patients to make informed decisions about their treatment options. By providing comprehensive information about the benefits, risks, and alternatives to medication, healthcare providers can help patients weigh the pros and cons of different treatment approaches and actively participate in their care. Psychoeducation also fosters medication adherence, self-advocacy, and resilience, equipping individuals with the knowledge and skills to navigate the challenges of living with a mental health condition.

In addition to medication management, holistic approaches to mental health care encompass a range of interventions, including psychotherapy, lifestyle modifications, peer support, and complementary therapies. Integrating these modalities into a comprehensive treatment plan addresses the multifaceted nature of mental illness and promotes holistic well-being beyond symptom management alone. By adopting a holistic approach, healthcare providers can tailor treatment strategies to address the unique needs and preferences of each individual, promoting recovery, and resilience across the lifespan.

Conclusion

Medications are valuable tools in the treatment of mental health conditions, offering relief from symptoms, preventing relapse, and improving overall functioning and quality of life. However, the use of medications involves careful consideration of the benefits, risks, and individualized needs of each patient. By fostering collaboration, assessment, education, and holistic care, healthcare providers can empower individuals to make informed decisions about their treatment options and achieve optimal outcomes in their journey towards mental health and well-being.

Introduction

In the vast landscape of mental health, individuals often find themselves navigating turbulent waters alone, struggling to make sense of their experiences and emotions. However, amidst the challenges, there exists a beacon of hope: support groups and communities. These sanctuaries of empathy and understanding provide solace and strength to those grappling with various mental health issues. In this holistic guide to mental health, we delve into the profound impact of support groups and communities, exploring how they foster healing, resilience, and solidarity among individuals facing similar struggles.

Understanding Support Groups

Support groups are safe spaces where individuals gather to share their stories, challenges, and triumphs with others who can relate to their experiences. These groups can take various forms, ranging from in-person meetings to online forums and virtual communities. What unites them is the shared goal of offering mutual support, validation, and encouragement to each member.

The Power of Shared Experiences

One of the most compelling aspects of support groups is the power of shared experiences. In these settings, individuals find comfort in knowing that they are not alone in their struggles. Whether it's coping with anxiety, depression, addiction, or trauma, members of support groups discover kindred spirits who understand the nuances of their journey. This sense of validation and connection can be profoundly healing, alleviating feelings of isolation and fostering a sense of belonging.

Breaking the Stigma

Support groups play a pivotal role in breaking the stigma surrounding mental health issues. By providing a platform for open dialogue and vulnerability, these communities challenge societal taboos and misconceptions about mental illness. Members feel empowered to share their stories authentically, without fear of judgment or shame. Through this collective effort, support groups contribute to a more inclusive and understanding society where mental health is recognized as a fundamental aspect of human well-being.

Embracing Empathy and Compassion

Empathy and compassion are the cornerstones of support groups and communities. Within these spaces, individuals offer each other unwavering support, listening without judgment and offering words of encouragement and validation. Through empathetic connections, members gain insight into their own struggles while also learning from the experiences of others. This exchange of empathy fosters a culture of compassion that transcends individual differences and fosters a sense of solidarity.

The Role of Peer Support

Peer support is a central tenet of support groups, where individuals draw strength from the wisdom and resilience of their peers. Unlike traditional therapy or counseling, which often involve interactions with professionals, support groups emphasize the power of peer-to-peer support. This dynamic allows members to share practical strategies, coping mechanisms, and insights gleaned from their own experiences. Peer support creates a collaborative environment where everyone has a voice and contributes to the collective journey towards healing and recovery.

Building Resilience and Coping Skills

Participating in support groups can significantly enhance individuals' resilience and coping skills. By engaging with others who have faced similar challenges, members learn adaptive strategies for managing stress, regulating emotions, and navigating difficult circumstances. Moreover, witnessing the resilience of fellow group members instills hope and optimism, reminding individuals that recovery is possible even in the face of adversity. Through shared experiences and collective wisdom, support groups empower individuals to cultivate resilience and embrace their journey towards mental well-being.

Fostering a Sense of Community

At their core, support groups are catalysts for building meaningful communities bound by shared experiences and mutual support. These communities provide a sense of camaraderie and belonging that is essential for mental health and emotional well-being. Members forge deep connections with each other, forming friendships that extend beyond the confines of the support group meetings. In times of distress or celebration, the support and encouragement of the community serve as pillars of strength, reinforcing the notion that no one is alone on their journey towards healing.

Navigating Challenges and Setbacks

While support groups offer invaluable benefits, they are not immune to challenges and setbacks. Group dynamics, differing perspectives, and conflicts may arise, requiring open communication and conflict resolution strategies. Additionally, individuals may experience setbacks in their recovery journey, encountering moments of doubt, relapse, or discouragement. However, it is precisely during these challenging times that the support of the group becomes most crucial. Through empathy, understanding, and unwavering support, members rally around each other, offering hope and encouragement in times of need.

Embracing Diversity and Inclusivity

Support groups thrive on diversity and inclusivity, welcoming individuals from all walks of life regardless of age, gender, ethnicity, or background. In these inclusive spaces, diversity is celebrated as a source of strength, enriching the collective experience and fostering empathy and understanding across different perspectives. By embracing diversity, support groups create an environment where everyone feels valued, respected, and heard, contributing to a more equitable and compassionate society.

The Evolution of Virtual Communities

In recent years, the landscape of support groups has expanded exponentially with the rise of virtual communities and online platforms. These digital spaces offer unprecedented access to support and resources, connecting individuals from around the world with shared experiences and interests. Virtual support groups provide flexibility and convenience, allowing members to participate from the comfort of their own homes while overcoming geographical barriers and logistical constraints. In an increasingly interconnected world, virtual communities serve as lifelines of support and solidarity for those in need.

Conclusion

Support groups and communities represent beacons of hope and healing in the journey towards mental well-being. Through shared experiences, empathy, and peer support, individuals find strength, resilience, and belonging in the company of others who understand their struggles. As we navigate the complexities of mental health, let us embrace the transformative power of community, recognizing that together, we can find solace, support, and strength in our shared humanity.

Chapter 17. Holistic Practices for Mental Well-Being
Yoga, Meditation, and Mindfulness

Introduction

In today's fast-paced world, where stressors seem to lurk around every corner, the quest for mental well-being has become paramount. As we navigate through the complexities of modern life, holistic practices offer a beacon of hope and a path towards inner peace. Among these practices, yoga, meditation, and mindfulness stand out as powerful tools for nurturing mental health and fostering overall well-being.

Understanding Holistic Health

Holistic health emphasizes the interconnectedness of mind, body, and spirit. It recognizes that mental well-being cannot be achieved in isolation but requires a comprehensive approach that addresses various aspects of our being. Rather than merely treating symptoms, holistic practices aim to promote balance and harmony within the individual.

The Essence of Yoga

Yoga, originating from ancient India, is more than just a physical exercise regimen; it is a holistic discipline that unites the body, mind, and breath. Through a series of postures (asanas), breathing techniques (pranayama), and meditation, yoga offers a profound means of self-exploration and self-transformation.

The practice of yoga cultivates awareness of the present moment, allowing individuals to observe their thoughts and sensations without judgment. This heightened awareness fosters mindfulness and helps alleviate the grip of stress and anxiety. Moreover, yoga promotes physical strength, flexibility, and balance, contributing to a sense of vitality and well-being.

The Power of Meditation

Meditation, often regarded as the cornerstone of mindfulness practices, entails the deliberate focus of attention to induce a state of mental clarity and emotional calmness. By training the mind to anchor itself in the present moment, meditation enables individuals to disengage from the incessant chatter of the mind and find refuge in stillness.

Various meditation techniques exist, ranging from mindfulness meditation, where one observes the flow of thoughts and sensations, to loving-kindness meditation, which cultivates feelings of compassion and goodwill towards oneself and others. Regardless of the method employed, meditation empowers individuals to develop resilience in the face of adversity and to embrace life with equanimity and acceptance.

Cultivating Mindfulness

Mindfulness, often synonymous with present-moment awareness, entails paying deliberate attention to one's thoughts, feelings, and bodily sensations without attachment or aversion. Rooted in Buddhist philosophy, mindfulness encourages individuals to embrace each moment with openness and curiosity, recognizing that every experience, whether pleasant or unpleasant, is an opportunity for growth and self-discovery.

Mindfulness practices range from formal meditation sessions to informal daily activities such as mindful eating, walking, and breathing. By incorporating mindfulness into their lives, individuals can enhance their capacity for self-regulation, emotional resilience, and empathic attunement. Moreover, mindfulness fosters a deep sense of connection with oneself, others, and the world at large, fostering a profound sense of belonging and interconnectedness.

The Science Behind Holistic Practices

While the benefits of yoga, meditation, and mindfulness have been extolled for centuries, modern science has begun to unravel the underlying mechanisms through which these practices exert their therapeutic effects. Neuroscientific research has demonstrated that regular meditation can remodel the structure and function of the brain, promoting neuroplasticity and enhancing cognitive functioning.

Moreover, mindfulness-based interventions have been shown to alleviate symptoms of depression, anxiety, and chronic pain while enhancing subjective well-being and quality of life. From reducing inflammation at the cellular level to modulating stress response systems, holistic practices exert a myriad of physiological and psychological benefits that transcend conventional medical treatments.

Integrating Holistic Practices into Daily Life

Incorporating yoga, meditation, and mindfulness into one's daily routine need not be daunting or time-consuming. Simple practices such as conscious breathing, gentle stretching, and moment-to-moment awareness can be seamlessly woven into the fabric of everyday life, infusing each moment with a sense of presence and vitality.

Setting aside dedicated time for formal practice, whether it be a brief meditation session in the morning or a rejuvenating yoga class in the evening, can serve as a sanctuary amidst the chaos of daily life. Moreover, cultivating mindfulness in mundane activities such as washing dishes or walking in nature can transform routine tasks into opportunities for reflection and renewal.

The Journey Towards Wholeness

Embarking on the journey towards holistic health requires courage, commitment, and self-compassion. It entails embracing the full spectrum of human experience, from moments of joy and connection to periods of sorrow and uncertainty. Through yoga, meditation, and mindfulness, individuals can cultivate the resilience and inner resources needed to navigate life's inevitable challenges with grace and equanimity.

In essence, holistic practices offer a gateway to self-discovery and self-transcendence, inviting individuals to embark on a journey of inner exploration and transformation. By honoring the interconnectedness of mind, body, and spirit, we can cultivate a deep sense of well-being that permeates every facet of our lives, fostering harmony and wholeness within ourselves and the world around us.

Conclusion

In a world characterized by uncertainty and upheaval, the quest for mental well-being has never been more pressing. Yoga, meditation, and mindfulness offer timeless wisdom and practical tools for navigating the complexities of modern life with grace and resilience. By embracing these holistic practices, individuals can embark on a journey of self-discovery and self-transformation, cultivating a deep sense of inner peace and well-being that radiates outward to benefit all beings. As we honor the interconnectedness of mind, body, and spirit, we pave the way for a more compassionate and harmonious world, rooted in the timeless wisdom of holistic health.

Introduction

In the journey towards achieving better mental health outcomes, advocacy and policy play pivotal roles. These aspects not only shape public perception but also determine the accessibility and quality of mental health services. As we navigate the complexities of mental health challenges, it becomes increasingly evident that effective advocacy and policy frameworks are essential for creating supportive environments and fostering meaningful change.

Understanding the Landscape of Mental Health Advocacy

Mental health advocacy involves raising awareness, challenging stigma, and advocating for the rights of individuals living with mental health conditions. It encompasses a range of activities, including public education campaigns, lobbying for policy reform, and providing support to those affected by mental illness. Advocates work tirelessly to promote understanding and acceptance, combat discrimination, and ensure that mental health remains a priority on local, national, and global agendas.

One of the most significant hurdles in mental health advocacy is combating the persistent stigma surrounding mental illness. Despite progress in recent years, misconceptions and negative attitudes continue to perpetuate barriers to treatment and support. Advocates strive to challenge these stereotypes, promote empathy and understanding, and empower individuals to seek help without fear of judgment or discrimination.

Advocacy efforts extend beyond challenging stigma to addressing systemic issues within healthcare systems and broader society. This includes advocating for increased funding for mental health services, improving access to care in underserved communities, and integrating mental health education into schools and workplaces. By advocating for policy changes and resource allocation, advocates strive to create environments that promote mental well-being and provide equitable access to support services for all individuals.

The Role of Policy in Shaping Mental Health Services

Policy frameworks play a critical role in shaping the provision of mental health services and support systems. From legislation governing insurance coverage to regulations governing mental health facilities, policy decisions have far-reaching implications for individuals seeking treatment and support. Effective mental health policy requires collaboration between policymakers, mental health professionals, advocacy organizations, and individuals with lived experience of mental illness.

One of the primary goals of mental health policy is to ensure parity between mental health and physical health services. Historically, mental health has been marginalized within healthcare systems, leading to disparities in access to care and treatment options. Policy initiatives aimed at achieving parity seek to address these disparities by mandating equal coverage for mental health services, including therapy, medication, and hospitalization.

Another key aspect of mental health policy is the promotion of early intervention and prevention strategies. By investing in programs that promote mental well-being and address risk factors for mental illness, policymakers can reduce the prevalence and severity of mental health conditions over time. This may include funding for school-based mental health programs, workplace wellness initiatives, and community outreach efforts aimed at reducing stigma and promoting help-seeking behavior.

In addition to promoting access to care and prevention initiatives, mental health policy also plays a crucial role in protecting the rights of individuals with mental illness. This includes legislation governing involuntary commitment, guardianship, and access to legal representation for individuals experiencing mental health crises. By enacting laws that uphold the dignity and autonomy of individuals with mental illness, policymakers can help mitigate the harmful effects of discrimination and ensure that all individuals receive the support and care they need.

Challenges and Opportunities in Mental Health Advocacy and Policy

While progress has been made in advancing mental health advocacy and policy, significant challenges remain. Limited funding, fragmented healthcare systems, and entrenched stigma continue to hinder efforts to improve mental health outcomes. Advocates must navigate complex political landscapes and competing priorities to effect meaningful change.

Moreover, the intersectionality of mental health with other social determinants, such as poverty, homelessness, and discrimination, underscores the need for comprehensive, multi-sectoral approaches to advocacy and policy.

Addressing the root causes of mental health disparities requires collaboration across disciplines and sectors to address systemic inequities and promote social justice.

Despite these challenges, there are also opportunities for progress and innovation in mental health advocacy and policy. Advances in technology have opened new avenues for outreach, education, and support, allowing advocates to reach broader audiences and engage with communities in new ways. Social media platforms, online forums, and digital storytelling have emerged as powerful tools for amplifying voices, challenging stigma, and fostering connections among individuals with shared experiences.

Furthermore, increased recognition of the importance of mental health in overall well-being has led to growing momentum for policy reform and investment in mental health services. Governments, philanthropic organizations, and grassroots movements are increasingly prioritizing mental health as a public health issue, driving investments in research, treatment, and prevention initiatives.

Moving Forward: Towards a More Inclusive and Supportive Future

As we look to the future of mental health advocacy and policy, it is clear that collective action and collaboration are essential. By working together to challenge stigma, promote access to care, and advocate for policy reforms, we can create more inclusive and supportive environments for individuals living with mental illness. This requires a commitment to listening to diverse perspectives, centering the voices of those with lived experience, and advocating for policies that promote equity, dignity, and social justice.

In conclusion, mental health advocacy and policy are integral components of efforts to improve mental health outcomes and create more supportive communities. By challenging stigma, promoting access to care, and advocating for policy reforms, we can build a future where all individuals have the opportunity to thrive and live full, meaningful lives. As we continue on this journey, let us remain steadfast in our commitment to building a more compassionate and inclusive world for individuals affected by mental illness.

"A Holistic Guide to Mental Health" provides a comprehensive exploration into the complexities of mental well-being, delving into various aspects from historical contexts to contemporary therapeutic approaches. From understanding common disorders like anxiety and depression to navigating relationships and advocating for better support systems, each chapter offers invaluable insights into the multifaceted realm of mental health. Readers will journey through chapters on genetics, childhood mental health, therapeutic interventions, medication management, and holistic practices, gaining a deeper understanding of the interplay between genetics, environment, and mental wellness. With a focus on destigmatization and empowerment, this book equips individuals with the knowledge and resources to navigate their mental health journey with resilience and compassion.

ABOUT THE AUTHOR

Mr. C. P. Kumar is a retired Scientist 'G' from National Institute of Hydrology, Roorkee, Uttarakhand, India. He is also a Reiki Healer and Chakra Balancing practitioner (with pendulum dowsing) and offers Emotional Freedom Technique (EFT) to help individuals with emotional issues. Mr. Kumar has authored many books on technical, spiritual, and social topics.

For further details, you may visit his webpage
https://www.angelfire.com/nh/cpkumar/virgo.html